T0146556

LET GOD
Rub You the Wrong Way

VERNESSA Y. FOUNTAIN

authorHOUSE®

AuthorHouse™
1663 Liberty Drive
Bloomington, IN 47403
www.authorhouse.com
Phone: 1 (800) 839-8640

© 2017 Vernessa Y. Fountain. All rights reserved.

No part of this book may be reproduced, stored in a retrieval system, or transmitted by any means without the written permission of the author.

The Authorized (King James) Version of the Bible ('the KJV'), the rights in which are vested in the Crown in the United Kingdom, is reproduced here by permission of the Crown's patentee, Cambridge University Press.

Published by AuthorHouse 02/11/2017

ISBN: 978-1-5246-6922-5 (sc)
ISBN: 978-1-5246-6920-1 (hc)
ISBN: 978-1-5246-6921-8 (e)

Library of Congress Control Number: 2017901335

Print information available on the last page.

Any people depicted in stock imagery provided by Thinkstock are models, and such images are being used for illustrative purposes only. Certain stock imagery © Thinkstock.

This book is printed on acid-free paper.

Because of the dynamic nature of the Internet, any web addresses or links contained in this book may have changed since publication and may no longer be valid. The views expressed in this work are solely those of the author and do not necessarily reflect the views of the publisher, and the publisher hereby disclaims any responsibility for them.

Foreword

From counterweights to counterbalances, from counter-intelligence to the issue of diametric opposition, from hot to cold and going from the concept that purports that opposites attract to that of the challenge of being either big or small, from yin to yang and back, our world is full of opposites and extremes. When we apply our logic to the complexities of living a human existence far away from our Creator God and Father, the equation can become blurred. Why? Because the process used to analyze and systematically understand our life situation may not always be available or seemingly attainable.

In comes the Reverend Vernessa Fountain, with cape unfurled and moving at breakneck speed. Father God sends her just in time to rescue us through this, her first literary undertaking—*Let God Rub You the Wrong Way*!

It is, without doubt, a most difficult thing to humble oneself under the mighty hand of God, especially if no one ever stops to teach us about the greatness of our God, the wonder of His inexhaustible love, and the majestic and multilayered plan of redemption already set in place for the glorious purpose of assisting the Holy Spirit in returning us to right relationship with the Father. Once we are made aware of these things, our perspective on life improves, and we can then begin to see our value and purpose the way God wanted for us! Reverend Fountain does a fantastic job of graciously reminding us of that revelation, and she does it through her eloquent style of introducing theological truths by way of her storytelling skills!

I had the fortunate pleasure of having met Vernessa through my wife, Reverend Pastor Debra L. Matthews, whom I met in the early 1990s. Vernessa was one of my wife's mentees and support workers as my wife traveled in ministry throughout the East Coast of the United States. From the very start, Vernessa exemplified a woman of fashion, flair, fun, and spiritual fervor! She was always respectful of others and honorable in our deportment. I am honored to call her my sister!

Concerning Vernessa's authorship style for this book, the scale and dimension of Reverend Fountain's approach to her subject matter is broad, causing us to stop and rethink the process that God initiates in order to bring us into proper alignment with His will for our lives. Evangelist Fountain's sweet personality shines through the fluidity of her presentation as she allows the innocence and transparency of her own life journey to help us navigate the often dangerous and unforgiving turbulent waters of life.

Soft warning, though: this book will take you on a journey within the deep recesses of your soul to expose whether your motives in life are right or wrong. In either case, I need you to know one thing—everyone's carpet needs a good cleaning every now and then! Grace and peace be multiplied to your account. — Bishop Dr. Andre E. Matthews

PREFACE

This project is the result of an assignment that God gave me through a dream. Fear and doubt caused me to put it off for a long time because the task seemed to be so overwhelming that I didn't know how to go about fulfilling it. Perhaps, I procrastinated because I felt skeptical, unsure of whether or not the book would be a success. I wanted to be sure that it made the necessary impact, and before I realized it, time had quickly slipped away. It was as though I needed God to come down, part the waters, and tell me, "Thou shall write a book" before I could actually write it! I doubted my ability to carry out the task because I lacked the discipline and structure it required. All I had was what God had given me, and hindsight now tells me that was enough! My due date for publishing this book came and went because I allowed every excuse in the world to hinder me, almost to the point of having a spiritual stillbirth.

Many of my confidants and colleagues told me that this book was inside of me, and were holding me accountable for bringing it to fruition. Yet, for whatever reason, no call to action had taken place on my part. My lack of persistence had prevented me from going to the next level. Like the purification of gold, I sensed that God wanted to burn out the unwanted impurities. Fear, doubt, and to some degree, disobedience, were the irritants that would have to be removed before this assignment could be carried to full term.

It is His touch that navigates and propels us toward our destiny, but it also requires us to be obedient, with practical application of His Word. Then, we will be able to overcome the failures of life's experiences. The lost and dying need what God had deposited into me, but first I needed to empty myself out on paper for them to receive it.

I know we use the phrase "It takes a village to raise a child" with the understanding that it takes many outside the circle of just mom and dad to love, nurture, guide, discipline and rear a child. Well, who knew that it would also take a village to write this book? I would like to dedicate this book to the following people:

First, my mother, Azalee Fountain: my greatest cheerleader who instilled in me a desire for excellence in my early years. She would say: "Don't bring me incorrect homework." So, I would check, recheck, and recheck all my homework once more before showing it to her. It made me proud to find a mistake before I handed it to her. Many years later I learned that she probably wouldn't have known if my homework was right or wrong. For that, I say thank you, Mom. I'm still looking to correct the mistakes today because of the pride I take in my work.

Second, my spiritual mother, Geraldine Wright: It seemed that God knew that I was going to need a lot of moms in my life. Trust me, even today, I am not running short on moms. Mother Wright kept me grounded and focused and helped me learn how to maneuver through negativity without becoming negative. Above all, the greatest thing she showed me was my need to allow God to deliver me from people. I gained confidence and learned through His Word that I was who God said I was, and not what *people* said I was. For that I say thank you, Mother Wright.

To my sister Rhonda, and brothers Gregory, William and Christopher: I love you all and am so very proud to be your sister. Your strength means everything to me. To the Wright/Smith family, my extended family: thank you for your encouragement and finally officially adopting me into the family.

To First Lady Ty Hurt who gave me the push to PUSH. Here is the result. Thank you!

To Pastor Deborah Jones Matthews who was a mentor in the early stages of my ministry calling me "Evangelist" when I couldn't see it. Look at me today! Through her, I met Bishop Andre Matthews and together they have been a constant and stable hand in my ministry. For that, I will eternally be grateful.

To a God sent woman, Valerie Rocha: an author in her own right who met me at a conference and said: "I believe God is leading me to help you with your book." And that she did for months, until we finally produced a manuscript. That feeling, I shall never forget!

To Evangelist Sonya Bradford: Everyone should have a correction rod in their life. I say this with much love, for she has been a great supporter of my ministry and that rod of correction to which I will be forever thankful.

To Reverend Kasundra Brown-Corbin, who has been a friend till the end. I thank her for her words of encouragement. Whenever I thought I couldn't do it, or didn't have it in me, she would say: "I have every confidence in you." You'll never know how much that meant to me. Thank you.

To my church family, State Temple Church of God in Christ: you are the greatest church family ever, and I thank you for your motivation. To a daughter that wishes to be nameless, your consistent support behind the scenes is invaluable. To Prophetess Deborah Jones, my twin sister, thank you for the cover idea. There are so many other names to add that I just don't have room to list. To everyone else who encouraged me and said: "You can do it," who told me: "It's not too late," who told me to "Push!", those who prophesied to me and labored with me all through my craziness, I'm so grateful for all of you, and to all of you I say THANK YOU.

Let God Rub You the Wrong Way! Every irritant that is removed from our lives is replaced with blessings and spiritually healthy things that are needed to help us grow. The process is not pleasant or easy, but the end result is always worth the pain that is endured. As you read my story, see yourself birthing what God has placed in you! Commit to being disciplined, dedicated, and willing to be molded for the glory and perfection of God. I encourage you to be real with who you are and where you are. Allow God to do with you what He desires, and when you do, I guarantee you will love the end result!

CONTENTS

CHAPTER 1

Rubbing Us the Wrong Way

Several years ago, the Lord woke me up one morning from a deep sleep. As I sat on the side of the bed attempting to recall the dream I'd had, I began to reflect and was shown a piece of carpet. It appeared as any other ordinary piece of carpet, but when I took a closer look, I noticed that the nap of the carpet had been flattened from wear and tear. And then I saw several pairs of feet walking on the carpet. At that moment God asked me, "What do you see?" To me, there was nothing out of the ordinary that stood out. Being the visual person that I am, I wondered if this was a trick question because I saw nothing other than the feet walking across the carpet. At that moment, God showed me another piece of carpet. This piece of carpet looked brand new or like a piece of carpet that had been vacuumed. The nap stood straight up, and the same feet also walked over this piece of carpet. However, this time I could see footprints where the carpet had been walked on.

I'm searching for one spot.

There was not a place that the feet had walked across and had not left a footprint. Again, God asked me the same question: "What do you see?" This time I responded that I saw footprints on this piece of carpet, but I told God I saw none on the first piece. God explained that the carpet represented the lives of his people; the first piece of carpet represents where His people are now. "The feet represent me walking in their lives." Now I started to process the whole thing. At first, I was clueless and asked God to help me understand what was being said. *The carpet is the people of God. The feet are God.* Okay so far. After taking a closer look, I could see that the nap of both pieces of carpet had a long, shaggy texture. When new, the texture of the carpet would have been quite plush; however, I could tell that the first piece had acquired some wear and tear. The nap was much flatter and was not plush at all. God said, "I'm walking up and down in the lives of my people, and I don't see my footprints anywhere in their lives. I'm searching for one spot. I've walked all four corners of their lives, and I still can't find my footprints.

"The second piece of carpet represented the lives of my people when they first gave me their lives," He continued. "Every place I walked in their lives I could see my footprint. I walked all four corners, and I saw my footprints every time." Now I began to ponder some more. The first piece of carpet represented where we are now, but it showed no footprints. The second piece of carpet represented how we were when Christ first came into our lives and showed his footprints. Doesn't something seem wrong with this picture? Wouldn't you figure that the longer you've been with the Lord, the deeper the relationship would be? The answer depends on the amount of effort you apply to the relationship.

The More of God

Ideally, the amount of time you spend with God should create a quality relationship. You come to realize that the more you've made God the Lord of your life, the more you understand that you can't function properly without Him. It's at this point of spiritual awareness that you need "the more of God" to experience deeper fulfillment in your life. Wouldn't you think that God could find His footprints in that type of life? But God said, "No, let me tell you why. I don't see myself or my footprints in the lives of those who have walked with me for some time because of one word—*mediocrity*. Mediocrity has entered my body [the church], and it's destroying it." It is impossible to experience the more of God to the degree that He desires when you are living at a level of mediocrity. I will discuss in greater detail the importance of rising above average in the following chapters. For now, allow me to use this analogy. Before we were saved, our carpets (our lives) really looked a mess. Sin had left large stains all over our carpets. We were in such bad shape that if someone had given us a carpet in this condition, we would have been highly insulted. Keeping it wouldn't have been a second thought; we would have immediately thrown it away. Before we were redeemed by the blood of Christ, many of us had been thrown away like that worn and stained piece of carpet. How amazing is it that God, being the loving

Father that He is, would take another person's piece of garbage and restore it back to its priceless value! If you allow Him to, God will take your old, tattered carpet and make it new again for the glory and edification of His kingdom.

The journey to spiritual cleansing is a process. Each level of purification allows us to rise above the standard of mediocrity. What I love about God is that He always knows how to get the best out of us. We should be so happy with what God has done in our lives. Others hardly recognize the new creatures that we've become, and if the truth be known, we hardly recognize ourselves.

God says, "Do." We say, "Yes, Lord!"

God says, "Go." We say, "I'll go!"

God says, "Jump." We say, "How high?"

God says, "Speak." We say, "I'll speak for you!"

The Lord longs for those days again—the days when whatever He asked of His people, they were eager and willing to fulfill it. It would appear that those days are long gone as a result of mediocrity.

CHAPTER 2

Giving God Our Leftovers

Today, God says that we have become like that first piece of carpet. We go through the motions of perpetuating the claim that we have the perfect testimony of running with God to see what the end will be. But, in essence, all of our actions reflect a different sentiment—"I'm a little tired now, so I'm just going to take a nap and rest a while. I'll pick up where I left off in my journey after I rest. The journey is long and tiring; besides, I've got plenty of time." We are under our false assumption that we have a close relationship with Jesus. The Enemy has coerced us into thinking that God will allow us to cash in the blessings despite not following any of the commandments He has given. We take for granted that we will not miss the opportunity to get caught up in the rapture. We use the excuse that God understands that we are humans who need to get whatever is holding us up out of our system. And then, we will give God our full attention. We have no concept of regret or lack of integrity when it comes to our servitude. My all-time favorite line is, "God knows my heart." We really don't believe that God knows our hearts, because if we did, our hearts would be filled with fear and reverence.

> *The creation* **can** **never** *be more*
> *or know more than*
> *the Creator.*

This is dangerous ground because God's word tells us that no individual knows the day or hour when the Son of Man shall appear—not even the angels (Matt. 24:36). It's as though we have become an insane people. We have slipped into thinking that God is just thrilled over whatever quality of service we give Him. We act more sensibly with and give our natural supervisors more respect than we give God. Shamefully, when it comes to the God of creation, we act as though we, the creation, know more than the Creator. The truth of the matter is that the creation *can never* be more or know more than the Creator.

Being caught getting ready will not yield the same results as *being* ready. Because of our sinful nature, we seem to function better when we have a visible supervisor. We would never even consider pulling anything like this with a human overseer unless we were insane. We make the mistake of assuming that because God is not visible to the naked eye, we can act like He doesn't see us. Psalm 113:5–6 (NIV) says, "Who is like the Lord our God, the One who sits enthroned on high, who stoops down to look on the heavens and the earth?" He sees all and knows all, and yet the mighty God of creation receives less respect than the creations. Yes, some regard should be given to those who have natural authority over you. Give Caesar what is his and give God what belongs to Him as well (Mark 12:17). This means your time, your finances, and all of *you*. With great reverence, you should be mindful to *fear* the one who has the ability to alter all aspects of your life, not just life itself. We are content with giving God whatever we feel at that moment, never considering that He never gives us leftovers. He loves us enough to give us the best even when we do not deserve it.

Allow God to remove the stains of sin from your life. Fight past the commonality of being mediocre! The power of God can transform your life and maintain your spiritual sanity. There is a way that seems right when serving God, but without continual cleansing of those things that cause your life to be stained, God will never be able to see His footprint. Getting by with just a little of Jesus will continue be the status quo in your life. You will never experience who He wants to be in your life the way He desires to abide in your life without this cleansing.

CHAPTER 3

The Mark of Excellence

In chapter 1 we discussed the importance of rising above mediocrity. Now let's take it a bit further and identify what the mark of excellence looks like. As I mentioned earlier, we tend to give respect to our human superiors more than giving God the reverence that He's due. Isn't it funny how the presence of a supervisor can call our actions to attention and push us to strive for the mark? What mark am I referring to? I'm making reference to the mark or level of excellence that is required in our everyday lives to serve God and His people. During an average workweek, we give our jobs forty or so hours. They may be physical hours; however, that does not mean that they are *productive* hours. Let's break it down a bit further. In a normal workday, a person supposedly works nine hours, not counting lunch and two fifteen-minute breaks. Therefore, in actuality, the required work time comes out to seven and a half to eight hours a day. This does not include the variables such as illness, moods, the weather, and so on that affect the quality of work performed in this time frame. Some days, you know you have given your best, at 100 percent, and other days it may seem as if you've worked twelve hours and only given 50 to 60 percent of yourself. This is another example of *average*—not exceptional or surpassing, even though it is our reasonable service. We don't implement extra in anything unless there is something lucrative in it for us.

Like children who have been caught with their hands in the cookie jar, the thought or threat of our supervisors correcting us forces an attempt to correct the problem ourselves. For example, you're usually on time for work, and know you need to be there by eight o'clock in the morning. For the past five days, you've been late three mornings, coming in at eight thirty. On the inside, you're secretly asking for grace while hoping you don't get caught, and then you notice that your supervisor looks at you in a way that you perceive as "funny." If the truth be told, it could be that your conscience is getting the better of you. Fearfully, you think to yourself, *Uh-oh! She's getting ready to say something to me about being late. Next week I'll do better and get back on track.* Rather than facing the consequences, you make an attempt to be self-corrective. You go through the process of making the necessary changes before the issue has to be addressed.

Interestingly enough, we will give our supervisors the utmost respect for their authoritative roles but slight God because we can't see or perceive Him looking at us "funny." Therefore, we continue with business as usual. We become mediocre in our actions, allowing ourselves to become complacent. We take for granted and forget that God is more powerful than any natural supervisor; He's already aware and knows the intent of our actions before we do them. If we looked at ourselves realistically, we would know that there are some problems or issues that need correcting in our lives. It's true that life's circumstances can hinder us from reaching the mark of excellence in our Christian walk, but we cannot use this as an excuse to give God less. *I would give 100 percent, but if giving 50 percent is enough and no one challenges me to give more, then average is satisfactory,* we might think. I'm not merely referring to a job done poorly. God measures the level of excellence comparable to every man.It's possible that God qualifies what I do for Him as 100 percent while what you give Him is qualified at 50 percent to me but 100 % to God. How is that possible? Because it is the *quality* of service given and the *condition of the*

Let God Rub You the Wrong Way

heart that are the determining factors. Unfortunately, simply doing enough to get by is the mind-set that has crept into both our lives and the church.

Average keeps us from rising above the bar of excellence

Average and *mediocre* are so closely related and so well accepted because neither requires much from you. Average says, I'm giving the consistent norm. I could give above or give more however why would I "rock the boat". I'll give what is common or what is ordinary. Mediocre says I'm giving what I know is not satisfactory, might even be considered second rate or so-so. However the mind set or thought process that goes along with mediocre say "Well at least I'm giving something and something is better than nothing. I know a lot of people doing or giving nothing so God should be happy.

That's why it's so easy to justify saying, "Hey, at least I showed up. What more do you want?" as if we are doing God a favor. Disillusioned, we tell ourselves that half the battle was showing up and that God and whoever else should be glad that we're there. The fact that we actually worked is a bonus since we could have stayed at home. This is the mind-set and behavior that closes the door to our blessings, yet we will get mad and wonder why we are not promoted. Our average keeps us from rising above the bar of excellence.

Our level of excellence and our service to God cannot be measured against each other. They can only be measured by what God appoints each of us to do. Allow me to share this with you: my level of excellence and your level of excellence may be measured by two completely different sets of standards. You cannot hide behind the best of someone else or what we deem as their best. God tests our level of excellence against His word. The Bible tells us clearly that we should not be deceived, because whatever we put out for Him shall come back to us. (Gal. 6:7)

We know in our walk with the Lord whether or not we're striving to reach "the mark." It's true—we may not reach the mark every day, and believe me when I tell you that I'm thankful to God for grace during those times when we don't. Striving for excellence is not something that comes easy. To be honest with you, it requires a great amount of discipline. Nothing God does is average, and because He gave his best by giving us His son, He requires the best from us.

Unlike us, God never gets confused. But He doesn't want us to cheat Him either! What I love about God is that He is a good supervisor, one who will not leave us to our own devices. Since we can't fix our problems entirely by ourselves, He comes alongside us to help us rectify them. The much-needed help came through His Son, Jesus Christ, and it's through His death that the tough stains of sin are removed. And it's through

His blood that we become justified, enabling us to accurately measure up. Giving Jesus as a sacrifice to save us was the best that He had. Knowing this, how can we not want to give Him more?

Regardless of how long we've been in our walk, we are still required to endeavor toward the mark of excellence. (Phil. 3:14) God's word is true, and when we allow it to saturate our thinking, the irritant of complacency will be removed.

CHAPTER 4

Rising from Our Slumber

Why is it that we as Christians fall asleep spiritually so quickly? We could have just experienced an amazing move of God with deliverance taking place, yet soon after, something else will snatch our attention and we will be lulled back to sleep. We forget the miracles of God almost as soon as He performs them. How can we have a healthy relationship like this? The characteristics of having a healthy relationship with God are very similar to those in a natural relationship. In the beginning, everything is new and exciting. You can hardly wait to see the person and spend time with him or her. You want to spend every moment listening, sharing, and getting to know who he or she is. Likewise, it is the same with our spiritual relationship. We thank God for every little thing, right down to the bug on the sidewalk, regardless of how much we are going through. We are careful of how we speak to and treat others for fear of breaking God's heart. With excitement, we share with everyone we see who He is and what He has done. Thirsty for more, we spend late nights praying and reading His word to see what it says about our lives. We are fully alert and aware of the essence of our loved one.

It's time that we wake up and become alert to the will of God for our lives.

Over time, we begin to get comfortable with the relationship and start to take it for granted. Our intent was never to fall asleep or become lax with what God wanted us to do. Due to the spirit of human nature and life's circumstances, we become spiritually sluggish. We find ourselves like the disciples in the Garden of Gethsemane. Allow me to illustrate: understanding and accepting the grueling task that had been set before Him, Jesus asked the disciples to arise from their slumber and stay awake with Him, praying for one hour. Not fully comprehending in the Spirit what the Lord was asking of them, I'm sure each of them replied something like, "No problem. We've got your back, Jesus. After all, what's one hour?" Yet, we find that no sooner had Jesus made the request of His disciples than they unintentionally abandoned their watch and fell back to sleep. Jesus, knowing the outcome but still needing to fulfill scripture, awakened them once more. Apologetically, the disciples reassured Him that they had gotten enough sleep and would give Him their undivided attention by supporting Him in prayer. Once again, within a very short period of time into the watch, they were found in a deep sleep again. This time Jesus allowed them to sleep. It's time that we wake up and become alert to the will of God for our lives.

Mark 14:38 tells us to watch and pray so that we will not enter into temptation. Isn't it interesting that even the Son of God, who sits on the right hand of the Father, had to pray and seek God to avoid falling into the snares of temptation? Why do we think we can do less and still stay in the will of God? This scripture illustrates that to avoid the enticement of mediocrity and spiritual complacency, we have to stay spiritually alert. When you spend time with God, you will learn what His will is for your life. Your level of dedication to Him gives depth and meaning to the relationship. You learn what it will take to maintain a healthy relationship. When you sacrifice some of you, you will not be so quick to forget who He is and what He has done in your life. It's not enough to read or hear what is being said. We must *apply* the Word through daily practice so that the impurities that hinder us can be burned out.

> *... preparing your minds for action,*
> *and being sober-minded ...*
> **1 Peter 1:13a (ESV)**

When we become comfortable with the relationship, we do not apply the same diligence that is needed to keep us on course. This is where we enter into the danger zone, causing spiritual shame. God then has to use the very things that we have become familiar with, such as the cares of the world and various temptations, to catch our attention and to place us back on course. As we pray and seek God's face, it enables us to be spiritually aware, vigilant, and conscious of His voice. It is through the word that He prepares our minds for action and enables us to be sober-minded (1 Peter 1:13a). When we seek a relationship with the Savior and have the mind of Christ, we will be spiritually awakened, alerting us to a call to action so that we can fulfill the purpose of the Master.

CHAPTER 5

Matching Up

As believers, our lives can be challenging just trying to keep the vows that we made to the Lord and we thank God for His forgiveness when we fall. We are all called to witness to the lost. However, when you are in leadership/ministry and definitely in the eyes of people, every aspect of your life is under a magnifying glass. There is the expectation that you are to be perfect. Any mistakes you make can cause ridicule and severe judgment—intended or not. Those in leadership/ministry are sometimes not allowed to hurt or have problems nor is there safety in letting others know that there are hurts or problems.

God requires from us our total mind, body and soul. He wants all of us. We sometimes forget that that includes our will. When our will lines up with the will of God then we can give Him total obedience. It's very similar to being in the military. When you enter into boot camp, you no longer have rights. Your body, time, and freedom become the property of Uncle Sam. In an effort to break your will (Uncle Sam breaks your will, God asks you to surrender willing your will), you're inundated with a rigorous training regimen and intense mental conditioning as you are disciplined to pay close attention to detail when following orders. From the time you enter boot camp and through all the ranks, you develop a sense of trust and respect for your fellow comrades and your commander in chief. All of the training and skills you have cultivated will help you prepare for the darkest of situations when you are simply required to follow orders, no questions asked. Uncle Sam calls that being on a need-to-know basis. Your superiors decide what you need to know, not you.

Whether you are in the ministry or not, the same is true for you. God simply wants to know that you love Him enough to trust and obey. Let me express to you that you cannot trust and *not* obey. The two become synonymous. Your mental conditioning comes from memorizing scripture. (Ps.119:11), and the rigorous training comes when you develop methods to fast and pray effectively (Is. 58:6). Good mental conditioning comes when you can meditate on God (Rom. 12:2).

> ### *The loss of our purpose can be grounds for disaster if we do not stay rooted and grounded in the Word of God.*

It's important that you understand that you can obey and not trust. It's a matter of having respect for authority. We do that with law enforcement. When we get pulled over, the police officer asks us for our license and registration. We give the officer what he wants because of the power and authority he has, but that doesn't mean that we actually trust him. His position/ authority makes us feel uncomfortable. We may or may not have done anything wrong, either. It may be nothing more than a blown brake light, but the fact of who he is makes us feel uncomfortable and fearful. It's that respect for authority that calls us to attention. We may not trust him, but because of his authoritative role, we will *obey*. God wants us to trust and obey Him out of our love and respect for His authority. Galatians 6:3 says, "For if a man thinks himself to be something, when he is nothing, he deceives himself." We must fight against our inner selves and prevent them from becoming overly sensationalized and lost due to our pride and ungodly secret agendas. The loss of our purpose can be grounds for disaster if we do not stay rooted and grounded in the word of God.

Our relationship with God requires the same, if not more, discipline than being in the military. Yet, as we become lax, we feel like it really doesn't take all of that. His instruction is so vital to our success because having a structured regimen is needed to offset the insecurities and spiritual blemishes we acquire. We do a disservice to God and His people when we lose focus and get caught up with the fads of Christianity instead of meeting the needs of the body of Christ. It requires sacrificing all aspects of who we are toward the furthering of the kingdom of God. I guess one could say this is the ultimate goal. We must be totally sold out. Like any goal needing to be achieved, you have to break it down into smaller portions and be objective when assessing where you are and who you are as it relates to its accomplishment.

When we first come to the Lord, we are eager to please, fulfill, and do. With time, just like the carpet, we undergo not only spiritual but emotional wear and tear too. If the truth be told, we can do *nothing* without Him. We need the salvation and cleansing of God, if for no other reason than that we are prone to fouling up. Factor in human inadequacy, and it's a miracle that we can do anything worthwhile for God—not to mention our feeling of being so unworthy a vessel for His service yet being full of zeal to serve Him. Praise God that He has already factored in more than a sufficient amount of grace and mercy to offset our human deficiency. Indeed, He knows what it will take to match us up to *His* standards.

Finding My Pulse

In the early years of my Christian walk, I struggled with comparing myself to others in ministry who

I believed were mighty in the kingdom of God. I patterned myself after these people because I felt they captured the word of God in such a way that when I left their services, I felt spiritually enlightened. There are too many to mention, but like these mentors and role models, I wanted to make a difference in the lives of God's people.

So I took the necessary steps of learning how to pray, read, and apply His word to my life. Over time, what I came to realize is that the closer I became to God, the more obstacles and challenges I had to encounter. Through these struggles, I became vulnerable and transparent, allowing God to burn out layers of dross. And then one day I had a reality check. When you're younger, you feel like you have all the time in the world. It's funny how your perspective changes as you get older. I had been so busy living for God that I had never taken the time to reflect introspectively on what I had accomplished during the time I had been blessed to enjoy being on this earth. For me, this seemed to be a pivotal point in my life. I was going through a spiritual steam cleaning. God was teaching me how to match up to His standards by redefining my own.

It seemed as if I had been living blindly and had nothing to show for my life. To me, it appeared that there had been no significant contributions made on my part and nothing that stood out that I could attribute to my legacy or acclaim. Compared to the men and women of God who I felt was making an impact on the world, such as the T.D. Jakeses, Juanita Bynums, and Joyce Meyerses, I had very little—or so I thought. Falsely, I measured myself against others thinking this was the yardstick for my success. I was convinced that I had nothing. Thankfully, God corrected my bogus self-notions by sending another of my dear friends to remind me of the dangers of measuring myself against others. She encouraged me to measure by using God's word (Ps. 26:2) as my measuring stick. She listened to me whine about my lack of progress and the excuses I had given over the past several years regarding the completion of this book. After hearing me out, she responded by saying three simple but profound words: *"Just do it!"* She clearly asserted that if I would just buckle down and do what I needed to do, I could finish the project. Firmly but lovingly, she reminded me of my humble beginnings in ministry and pointed out that God knew exactly what He was doing as He developed the "evangelist in me," even if I didn't see it. What I find interesting is that she had no knowledge of the process I had to go undergo in my evolution. She remembered my early development and wanted me to celebrate who and where I was now.

Genuinely eager and happy to assist others with their ministry, "evangelist" had been the last thing I saw myself becoming. Reflectively, she helped put my focus back into proper perspective. I speak candidly when I say that I understand and realize beyond a shadow of doubt how blessed I am, and I'm forever grateful for each one of those blessings. Respectfully, I know that all that I have and will become is a result of God's favor on my life. When I allowed Him to rub out the things that were unpleasing to Him, He placed his seal of approval over me and promoted me to where I am today. I must confess that I was embarrassed because of my lack of belief in myself and the abilities that God had gifted me with. Again, I needed to be reminded to stay on track. It was important for me to know that I didn't need to compare myself to others. God will always and simply deal with us. Honestly, I had been encouraging others to let God flourish in their lives and fulfill the dreams He had placed in them when I wasn't even following my own advice. To add insult to injury, she implemented the tactic that every preacher, pastor, or clergymen dreads— reciting your own sermon back to you to drive the point home! When someone encourages you by using another preacher's sermon, it's no problem, but telling you to practice what you preach is like telling a doctor to follow his own prescription.

Since I had gotten so caught up comparing myself to everyone else, I was operating in a mode of mediocrity because my focus was on humankind and not God. When you pay attention to what God has to say about you and your situation, you can move and operate at the level of excellence He requires.

As I look back, I can now appreciate God's sense of humor, even though I still don't like having my own sermons preached to me! Do you see how easy it is to forget that the message is first to you and then out to the people? It was an effective method, and it produced the desired results. When we are in our cleansing and refining process, we often make the mistake of believing that we have to be like everyone else. We think that we lack value unless we have all the shiny trinkets or, as the kids say, "bling." I finally understood that comparing myself to someone else was like telling God that He didn't do a good job in creating me. Even though I had never verbally said this to God (I would probably need to be on medication to have said it), I was saying it with my actions. Besides, God knows my heart, so who was I fooling?

What I love about this is that as God deals with you and your impurities, He will sometimes use others to address them, and other times He will deal with you directly. These things may seem minute, but in the hands of the master, they are the tools He uses to remove the stains of sin that have been deeply embedded. One of the toughest challenges about comparing ourselves to others is that we will always fall short. The Enemy will always present us with a distorted image of who we are. God is the only one who can truly measure us, our gifts, and our talents according to His statutes. When we follow the blueprint of His word, we will always be accurately matched up to His standards.

CHAPTER 6

Spot Treatment Application

At the beginning of the book, as you recall, I expressed how I compared the various aspects of spiritual growth and fulfilling your purpose to the fabric and texture of a new carpet versus a worn carpet. The process that God takes you through can be a bit arduous, but in the end you will love the results. The determining factor is that you have to be willing to follow the instructions.

As I prepared mentally and spiritually to tackle this next phase of the journey, I continued to pray that God would help me stay on course. What I didn't realize was that God was already working it out on my behalf. I would like to introduce a friend, First Lady Ty Hurt, a pastor's wife who was instrumental in encouraging me to find time with God for this book. I will talk about our encounter in detail in another chapter, however the importance here is I was instructed to make an appointment with God. This appointment looked like it was going to be an early morning appointment. Let me start with the disclaimer that I am not—I repeat, I am not—a morning person. You know those blessed individuals who rise early so that they can read, clean the house, and do a load of clothes all before leaving to go to work while still feeling refreshed? Well, trust me, I'm not one of them! My pattern has always been to stay up until two or three o' clock in the morning to complete a job if necessary. When my head hit the pillow, I could sleep because I knew the job was done, and that was more important to me than getting sleep. Most times, I'd relish sleep so much that I would hit the snooze button at least four times before actually getting up.

Although somewhat subtle, changes were gradually being made. Despite the fact that I was incorrect in the process to acquire that time with God, providence finally kicked in. Slowly, I began to rouse at 6:00 a.m. without the use of an alarm clock. To me, this was a great turning point in my life because I no longer needed assistance getting up. I had been so bad that I had the type of alarm clock with dual alarms that married couples use, and I used both of them for myself with two different alarm times. As I moved through the process, it began to get easier, and I began praying immediately. And then one day after dinner, the voice of the Lord spoke to my spirit and said, *This is what you asked for*. In humble reverence, I replied, "Oh, Lord, you are so faithful to me, even when I don't always get things right."

Much like when we are trying to remove a stain from the carpet, there are certain instructions we must follow in order for the treatment to be effective.

Sometimes, depending on the type of stain, it can be removed with one treatment. Other times, the treatment has to be reapplied. Each time the carpet treatment has been applied, the carpet must be rinsed and then dried. The determining factor is that regardless of how many applications are applied, you have to follow the manufacturer's instructions to get the desired outcome. Even when we don't follow God's instructions the first time, He is patient with us and can still remove the stains from our lives when we finally correctly follow the instructions found in His word. Now, 6:00 a.m. has become my time to wait for the visitation of God. Every time He awakens me, it just reminds me of His faithfulness toward me.

I quickly realized that because the visitations were so early, I could no longer keep those late-night hours that I was once accustomed to. This major change had transpired in my life because of my hunger to be obedient and remain in the will of God. After dinner one evening, I remember telling First Lady Hurt that I could see that writing this book was going to change my entire life. This time, the smile remained, and I could sense her satisfaction in me for completing my assignment. How right I was: *it was about time I got something right!*

Spiritually impregnated with the dream to write this book, I found myself pregnant and past my due date. Like any pregnant woman past her due date, I just wanted it to come *out*! I didn't care what I had to do, I just wanted it out. So here I go—the contractions are getting stronger, and I'm *puuuuuuushing*!

There is no way to speed up the gestation process. Every phase must take its course because it has a purpose. Likewise, in each principle that God wants to impart to us, the lessons must be worked through and applied to allow His purpose for our lives to bring Him glory.

CHAPTER 7

Push Now

Every task given to fulfill our purpose requires a level of maturity. In the early stages of my ministry, I was full of zeal but lacked the structure and discipline needed to help me stay on task. Seeking God is good, but we still have to do our part in order for the vision to reach completion. Sometimes, even after we seek the will of God and He reveals it to us, we can still miss it.

He tries us again …

Several years ago, the Lord had given me a message entitled "It's Time to Push Now." The premise was based on how God had impregnated the church with His purpose, destiny, and word, and it was time to push in the spirit. As parents, we want a healthy, strong baby that's full of life. The worst possible thought would be to have a miscarriage or stillborn baby. However, there's another reality—dead or alive, you still have to push, and there's always a level of pain involved.

Each of us has been given a purpose and destiny to glorify God. In order for this to be fulfilled, we are required to seek His face concerning His will for our lives on a continual basis. We also need to allow the word of God to take root in our hearts, which will lead us to obedience and the strength to *push*. Even if a dream has been stillborn, maturity has taught me that it's not the end. It simply requires us to acknowledge our shortcomings and allow Him to take us through the healing process. Being a God of love and understanding, He *tries us again*. Therefore, our sincere prayer should be, "Lord, try me one more time. This time I will take better care of what you impregnated me with. My diet will be different, and I'll exercise my faith more and bring this baby to fruition."

To get a more vivid understanding and deeper meaning of what God was trying to reveal to me, I would like to re-introduce my friend, First Lady Ty Hurt, who had personal experience in giving birth both naturally and spiritually, since I had no personal experience to draw from. After listening, she began by asking me this question: "What does a mother do when she goes past her due date?" I responded, "I assume she would be very anxious, frustrated, and irritable." And then, she kept it real and made it plain: "Frankly, your claws are out and you are ready to lash out at others. For nine months you were in preparation with an expected end, the due date. Now that the day of arrival has come and gone, you've arrived at the 'any day now' point. This does not provide any comfort to you because you want that baby out *today*!"

First Lady Ty then went on to explain that I was in the "any day now" stage. She pointed out that the Lord had given me the vision several years earlier, and because I hadn't pushed through spiritually to the next level, I wasn't any closer to fulfilling my destiny. She reinforced my feelings and was accurate in identifying that I was at a point of frustration and needed to push the book out. As tears welled up in my eyes, she provided emotional support and comfort like a supportive midwife and declared, "We are going to touch and agree through prayer that this baby will come into fruition. God has other babies you need to birth, series and volumes, but you have got to get this one out before that can happen."

Although this was not what we were originally going to discuss, First Lady Hurt went on to say that she was mandated to help me by imparting instruction to me. "Find some time every day that you can go before the Lord and wait for His visitation. Don't be concerned about what you're going to write; just wait for the visitation." That required discipline, something that I didn't have a lot of in my life. The words rang so loud in my head that I could not ignore them. Isn't it just like us to think we hear so clearly yet still get it wrong and miss the point? Remember I told you in the previous chapter that I was incorrect in my process of acquiring time with God, this is what I meant.

Missing the Point

For the next two to three weeks I kept asking God what time of day and hour He would visit me when I should have just sat still and let Him do it. "Lord," I cried out, "give me the time and I will obey." And then one morning, He woke me up with prayer in my spirit. I got up and began to pray on the side of my bed, and in the middle of the prayer I got the urge to write! I looked around for the right something to write on and chose a steno book because all of the pages could easily be kept together. I wrote two pages, and I was never so happy about this number of written pages in my life! I rejoiced over this milestone for the next week and a half, relishing the time that God would come and visit me.

The next time First Lady Hurt and I were scheduled to fellowship, as we often did, I could hardly contain my excitement. I knew she wasn't expecting me to have started the book. I felt very proud of myself for having accomplished writing those two pages and wanted to surprise her. Trying to keep everything on the down-low, I proceeded to ask her as calmly as possible how everything was going with her at her church. Stealing my thunder, she immediately responded, "That's not what we came for!" I was immediately on the defense. I knew we would eventually get around to talking about me, but I was having issues with her stealing my moment, so I blurted out, "I started the book!"

It's our way of saying the problem is not us …

A lovely smile came across her face as I began telling her how I didn't have anything other than those two and a half pages that God had given me. Feeling satisfied with my progress and carrying out what I thought she had asked for, I told her how I was waiting on God to give me that special time of visitation. You know for God to shine a light from Heaven directly on me and say "write". I waited for her to continue to share in my elation. But her smile soon vanished, and I instantly knew I was in trouble. She looked me square in the eyes and said, "Did I tell you to do that?" At this point, I was having another moment and began thinking, *Okay, is she really tripping out? I know I did what she told me.* Isn't that how the conversation goes in your head? *I think I did what I was told to do,* as you second-guess it at the same time. Trying to recover from this emotional landslide, I started reading over what I had written and suggested that maybe I needed to make some changes. Again, she reiterated what she had said: "I told **you** **t**o pick a time that **you** would go before the Lord and *wait.* I didn't tell you to ask God what time He was going to get with you and visit. See, you've shifted all the responsibility on God and you feel you have none."

A lot of times we look for someone or something to shift the responsibility to. It's our way of saying the problem isn't us. Our thought process is, *Since I know it's not me, then it must be someone else or something else, and I need to find out what that someone or something else is.* This was my moment to understand that I hadn't done my part; meanwhile, God had remained faithful. He always does His part, but He will not do for us what He requires and knows we can do for ourselves. She went on to say that all I needed to do was just wait for God, and if He didn't tell me what time that would be—oh, well. Stunned, I sat there again, attempting to justify my actions. Listening to the tone of her voice, I could tell I was in trouble again. I silently pleaded with the Lord to help me catch on more quickly. In a loving but firm manner, the answer came back in the form of a purposeful rebuke. Suddenly, everything began to fall into place. What I needed was a crystal clear understanding of how to be disciplined and how to implement it.

I needed to practice organization and discipline on a daily basis and infuse them into every aspect of my life if I was going to get this book pushed out. I had to start from where I was since I was missing some of my earlier sermons (my car was broken into, and if you can you believe it, out of all the things I could have lost, my sermons were taken). I often laugh to myself and have said, "If I hear a phrase or a twist that reminds me of myself *anywhere*, I wonder if it was my work." Every message and all my notes would have to be outlined and organized in written form, preferably on a computer, if I was going to be able to stay on point. In order for me to deliver a healthy baby, I would have to take responsibility for staying fit, learning how to breathe, and preparing to push.

The point that I want to express here is this: even with the best intentions, we can still miss what is right in front of us. When God gives us something, it's up to us to follow through to full term. He will remain with us through each phase of the pregnancy and will even provide the strength to push; however, without a clear and defined plan of action, we are setting ourselves up for our dream and vision to be stillborn.

CHAPTER 8

Following the Blueprint

Sometimes, all of the ingredients to a great success story are there, but we don't recognize them. As I continued my journey in preparing for this book to be written, I had no idea how important following all of the steps to getting this project birthed would be. Much like being in the delivery room, I not only needed the midwife and a nurse but I also needed someone who could coach me to get this project completed.

Developing a successful blueprint
means just doing the simple things.

I remember an instance in which another dear friend and his wife, who are now pastors, shared a tidbit to help me in preparation for this project. They suggested that I needed to have all of my messages on a computer and to start a tape ministry. I informed him that my church didn't have a tape ministry, so he reiterated his point. He expressed that *I* was to start a tape ministry, not the church, defining the difference between what I needed and what the church could provide. Here was another example of not taking responsibility and using what someone didn't provide for you as an excuse for you to not do. Using something as basic as a micro recorder, which I already had but wasn't using for my benefit, would help me catalog my messages and organize my thoughts. Capturing the common thread throughout my sermons was the object of this lesson. I agreed to do it but expressed my dislike of having to listen to myself. I find that listening to myself is quite irritating because of the distinct, unusually sandy texture of my voice. Furthermore, because I am my own worst critic, watching myself would only lead to more embarrassment and was definitely out of the question. Once again, I saw that in hindsight I had missed the point because I was being ministry-oriented, which was good, but it wasn't what I needed to help me at the moment. What I needed was hands-on practicality. Part of developing a successful blueprint is just doing the simple things that are asked of you.

I prayed for God to help me, and again the answer came in the form of the reasoning behind the instruction. I was not to question, organize, or rethink my efforts. The simplicity came in merely doing. In fact, the exact words were to "just let it flow." Inspiration is not enough when you're fulfilling your purpose. In order to get the best results, you have to offset things like lack of organization and overcoming writer's block with the tools and resources that are provided.

Can you see a pattern in my life here? I wanted to please God and do His will, but I was missing the point. I could not help anyone until I had mastered and done the prep work for helping myself first. The problem was that the instructions were so simple and obvious that I was missing them. Sometimes in order for us to get the results required, we have to follow a blueprint. It was not enough to hear the instructions that would help me grow; I needed to pay close attention while I was doing them. The attention to detail was what I needed to perfect the task if I was going to move to the next level of ministry and purpose. In order to "just let it flow," I needed to do three things and no more: 1) meet with God in prayer every morning at the same time, 2) organize messages in one location, and 3) let my writing for the book just flow. At the end of the meeting, I left more determined than ever to stick to the blueprint and complete these assignments.

CHAPTER 9

Catalyst of Truth

Truth should always propel you to action (1 John 3:18). When we are in agreement with the will of God, His truth compels us to work things out when they are not in order. It is the agitating agent that will not allow you to sit idly. Truth tells you that you must move and can no longer remain in the place of complacency or disobedience.

Through our Savior we have spiritual liberty. It's this freedom that provides us with the avenue to connect with God. God's truth is always trying to connect with us. We are always given a choice. And although God is all powerful, He will not override *your* will. John 14:6 tells us that Jesus is the *way, truth* and *life*. God's word is the map that leads us to the path of life that brings us to a place of blessings. Obedience also provides a renewal of our souls, healing, and continuous new life.

When we choose to be totally committed and sold out, we submit our wills to the will of Christ.

Just as obedience and truth provide healing and renewed strength, the opposite can be said of disobedience. Because of our free will, we always have the choice to walk or not to walk in God's truth. When we do not take our relationship with Him seriously, it's easy for us to downplay His will for our lives. The older saints used to sing a song entitled "My Mind Is Gone." I would think, *Now, I understand some of the saints a little better. Some of them need to go back and get their minds wherever they lost them.* However, as I matured, I realized that wasn't the case. What the older saints were really saying was that they no longer had minds of their own. They had given up their minds, their ways of thinking, and their ways of controlling their wills. They chose to take on the mind and the will of Christ. Philippians 2:5 says, "Let this mind be in you, which was also in Christ Jesus." When we choose to be totally committed and sold out, we submit our wills to the will of Christ.

When we choose to be repetitively disobedient, regardless of the reason, our hearts are left hardened with residual layers of hurts, disappointments, and calluses from our poor decisions, causing us to be dull to the sensitivity of the Holy Spirit. I mentioned before that the Bible is our road map, but we really don't use road maps much anymore. Most of us have GPS. It's everywhere. It's in our cars and on our smartphones. The GPS system is very detailed; in fact, it will identify the names of the streets on the way to your destination before you even reach them. If you don't like tolls or the highway or simply want to take an alternate route, you have those options with GPS. The map that God gives us is not like GPS; we don't get to know the details upfront or what roads we will have to travel down to get to our destination. God expects us to follow and trust His word. Now, truth be told, the real reason we want to know the roads upfront is so that we can choose whether we want to take that route. If I have to go down Heartbreak Lane, Family Loss Circle, Illness Boulevard, Financial Distress Terrace, we may choose not to. We will just ask for another route and go another way. It would be nice, but that is not how life is. The road that has been chosen for each of us has been selected with each of us in mind, by the mind of God. The altered route will not lead you to the truth and you will end up at an altered destination. What's amazing is that we don't mind going where God has destined for us to go as long as we don't have to take the route He has chosen. I always say, you may not like the process or shall I say the route that God sometimes chooses but I guarantee you will love the end result or the final destination. Stay on course.

Because our Savior, Jesus Christ, shed his blood, we are sanctified in the truth (John 17:17). When truth begins to pull at your heartstrings, don't ignore the pull! Don't be insensitive to the spirit of God and act like truth couldn't possibly be talking to you. You may be asking yourself why God would want to have a relationship with you. Allow me to share this equation with you: truth + disobedience = a stony, hardened heart, which leads to wasted time.

It's going to cost all of you.

Through the sanctification and forgiveness process, our hearts can be made soft and pliable again, but at what cost to the individual? Actually, I'm going to tell you the cost: it's going to cost all of you. As I said earlier, you have to give up your mind to take on the mind of Christ. Don't believe the hype that you have plenty of time to live for Christ; *you don't have time!* One of the biggest lies that Satan has disillusioned the church into believing is that we've got plenty of time. He entices us with the sins of the flesh that Galatians 5:19–21 expresses, but we are also drawn away by our own devices, according to James 1:14, when we are not disciplined in applying the word of God to our lives. The Enemy persuades us to go on living our lives, using whatever lies necessary to lull us into a false sense of security; after all, you only live once. When you've finished living it up, then you can live for God—that is what Satan wants you to believe. No! Give God the best of your labor *now*, not when the devil has practically used you all up and you're just about crippled, deaf, and blind. Then, from a state of spiritual wreckage, you would talk about serving God? To make matters worse, we have allowed ourselves to spin so far out of control that when we do finally decide to serve God, we're exhausted and spiritually crippled from all the layers that have weighed us down.

When truth knocks, open the door to your heart and respond to it. Also never accept the hype that you are fine just the way you are. God always desires for us to do better. Yes, He accepts you the way you are when you come into a knowledgeable relationship with Him. That does not mean that you should stay that way or that He will leave you that way when you give Him complete control. Having a meaningful relationship with God requires a conscious effort.

This is not to say that you are going to do everything right all the time, nor does it mean that you should play with God. You cannot choose to stay with and live for Him for only two weeks and then decide to leave when things don't go your way. For a lot of us this is how we have handled our natural relationships and we attempt to bring this thinking over into our relationship with God. This does not work. I am referring to a relationship in which you surrender to His will for your life and experience the perseverance of His love. God's love is so powerful that when you come one way, you will always leave in a better position than you were in before you came.

When God looks upon us, He sees us as a completed work. Thus, unlike we who start many things but do not always follow through, God has the ability to complete the things that He begins regardless of how long they take, removing the layers of hurts and disappointments that life has left us. He continues to gently shape and mold our lives into the preordained destiny that has been set for us. It is through this process that God's spirit and the redeeming blood of Christ activates the catalyst of truth, moving us to obedience and enriching our relationship with God.

CHAPTER 10

A Working Relationship

It's human nature for us to want the best. We want to get into the best schools but don't like to study. We want the best jobs but don't have the necessary qualifications. We want the best homes even though we can't afford the house payments. We want the best relationships even though we may be emotionally broken. Regardless of the circumstances, qualifications, or requirements that we may or may not have, we always want the best but try to obtain them through second-rate means. Now logic tells us that if we put the best in, we will get the best out of what we are doing. However, we fail to apply that concept when it comes to God. Regarding God, something is wrong. We understand the principle of desiring the best quality, but for us it translates into our doing little but wanting more. Just like you have to apply yourself to get the best in life, you must apply quality effort to have a successful, working relationship with God.

A False Relationship

You cannot work your way to God. Isaiah 57:12 tells us that God will expose our righteousness and our works but that they will not benefit us. The prescription to having a healthy, meaningful relationship with God is clear: we have to draw close to Him, and He will draw close to us. We have to be cleansed and purified because our loyalty is divided between God and our worldly desires (James 4:8). Little time and service produce a little relationship. I am not talking about showing up to service, going through the motions, and thinking that we have fulfilled some requirement. Now, if we were being real with ourselves, we would need to admit that there are all kinds of reasons that we go through the process of "going to church and doing our Christian duty," such as self-betterment, wanting to have that "good feeling experience," shopping around for a spouse, and easing our conscience about the sin we have no intention of correcting unless we get caught. And afterward, we return to our status quo without any real change occurring in our lives. You can never, ever have a true experience with the Lord without your relationship with Him being changed for the better. Let me share this equation with you too: you, being godly sorrowful, with a *repentant heart* + *having a true experience with God* = ***a changed life***.

In 2 Chronicles 7:14, the important keywords are *pray, seek,* and *turn*: "If my people, which are called by my name, shall humble themselves, and *pray*, and *seek* my face, and *turn* from their wicked ways; then will I hear from heaven, and will forgive their sin, and will heal their land" (emphasis added). We have equated a repentant heart to mean saying we're sorry and adding some tears. Please don't misunderstand me—I'm not saying that godly sorrow will not produce tears or that telling God how sorry you are for having lived like you have is not important. However, none of that means anything without turning away from the life you lived. And I mean turning and going in the opposite direction. The Bible says that only when we humble ourselves (you might want to humble yourself before God does it for you), pray, seek God's face, and turn from our wicked ways will God forgive our sins and heal our land. Your heart is symbolic of your spiritual land as well as our physical land.

Your coming to terms with your sin cannot substitute any of the above components and still get the desired outcome. It's interesting how we substitute certain parts of the equation for our entire lives, never understanding why we never get the desired results. Instead of dealing with it, we play games with ourselves and God, hunching our shoulders, throwing our hands up, and asking what happened. Because God is gracious, merciful, and slow to anger (Ps. 145:8), we feel like "we're pulling one over on the *church,* when we are really cheating God. God's word and principles do not change and always require excellence. Whatever a man sows, that shall he also reap (Gal. 6:7). Therefore, the harvest that represents your time and service, whether lean or plentiful, will always come back to you in whatever form of quality you gave it. Remember, mediocrity is never going against the grain or rising above average. It's always going with the grain, doing what's comfortable and mundane, rather than giving your best effort. It causes us to have residual stains on our carpet.

Let's return for a moment to the two pieces of carpet. The reason God couldn't see His footprints in the old piece of carpet is because the nap of the rug was going in the same direction with the grain and had become flattened. When the carpet was brand new, the nap stood up straight, having a plush look. However, as the rug was left uncared for over time, it became embedded with dirt and stains, leaving the nap flattened in one particular direction or sometimes in several directions. In this condition, you can walk all over the rug but your footprints will not show. The carpet needs to be shampooed and vacuumed. Vacuuming alone is not sufficient as it will only cause the nap to stand but does nothing to remove the stains. How does this relate to you? Day-to-day living and circumstances produce wear and tear on your spiritual carpet. Certain situations may not pose a problem and can be dealt with quickly, like a quick spot treatment, while others may be more difficult and complex, causing our emotions to become entangled with stress, worry, and frustration. These situations require both a spot treatment and deep spiritual cleaning.

Anything that is unable to move forward will become stagnant.

Every challenge needs to be handled differently. When the root of the situation has not been dealt with, it causes us to be spiritually worn out until we are unable to identify the root cause and give up caring about how to rectify it. Putting forth any effort becomes so difficult that we become spiritually stuck. Anything that is unable to move forward will become stagnant, attracting more dirt.

The nap of a rug is made of millions of individual strands of wool. Individually, each strand stands alone, without significance, but together they form a beautiful rug. When we see the stains and dirt on carpet, it's unappealing to our eyes. But what we won't see unless we take a closer look is that the dirt attaches itself to each strand individually. Let's take a look at an example:

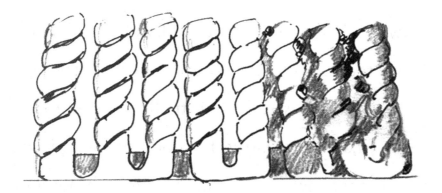

The image on the left is the clean fibers, and the one on the right is embedded with dirt. The purpose of frequent vacuuming and occasional shampooing is to remove the dirt and stains and return the carpet to its original state. The reason those early challenges in our Christian walk were not a problem is because we allowed God to spiritually vacuum and shampoo us right away. Our spirits always looked new and refreshed, and we took great pride in it. When we do not remain honest with ourselves and God, it will not take long for our spirits to become stained. We will never be delivered and free from the radicals of sin until the root of the matter is addressed.

CHAPTER 11

Debunking the Excuses

We can always find an excuse to not do something. At one stage in my life, I had a mind-set that said, "Today I'm full of excuses as to why I can't run the race that is set before me right now. This is not to say that I am not going to run again. It means I'm just a little tired, and I need to take a rest." There are two types of rest. The first is well deserved after working hard. The other kind is what you do right before you actually do any solid work because you are having a hard time getting started. This second type of rest is actually procrastination and is a great waste of time. I would really love to tell you that I have never been hoodwinked by procrastination, but the truth is that it has crippled all areas of my life at one time or another. However, I have learned from the consequences and now attack the root cause of it in my life—*fear*. When I didn't know how to handle a situation, I wouldn't do anything. It was as if to say that at some point I *was* going to know what to do. The truth was if I didn't know what to do at that moment, chances are I wouldn't know later on either unless God stepped in and gave me some direction. The results of doing nothing gradually set in, and I now realize that I had become worse off by feeding the fear, and it caused me to shut down. I had become completely immobilized. What a horrible state to be in.

I know I am not by myself. Perhaps this is one of the many reasons God inspired me to write this book, to help others who have allowed fear to rob them of time, sleep, finances, self-worth, and a meaningful relationship with God, just to name a few. God has poured so much into us as vessels, and for many of us it is now time for the *outpour* to be imparted. God has invested in us and desires to see a return. Between fear and mediocrity, it is a wonder that God can get anything constructive out of us at all. God doesn't want our excuses; He is looking for sincerity of heart and a willing servant. We must learn to take responsibility for our spiritual decisions and replace the average mind-set with good spiritual habits like memorizing and applying the word and remaining sensitive to the Holy Spirit.

God is like that shareholder, only better.

I'm not an expert on stocks and bonds, but I do know that if you invest your money in something, you do so with the expectation of a return that is usually greater than the original investment. A dividend is a distributed portion of a company's earnings paid on a regular basis (usually quarterly) by the shareholders out of their profits. God is like that shareholder, only better. He does not wait or withhold our blessings quarterly. He blesses us continually. The impartation of the spirit of God and *outpour* is all part of your purpose. Although we are part of the purpose, it is not entirely about us. I love the way the Lord does things. While we are about purpose and helping others, God fulfills us in the process. He increases our spiritual, emotional, and financial dividends because of our obedience. His faithfulness is always full and abounding. He is the optimum shareholder because if we take the focus off of "me" and place it on doing His will, the return is not only great but above what we could ever ask or think of (Eph. 3:20).

In closing, it is God's word that we are to use as our spiritual measuring stick, not humans' opinions.

Mediocrity is our greatest enemy and will always put us in a state of spiritual slumber. The world and church can be full of false expectations; therefore, we should strive to meet God's expectations to have a solid spiritual reality of who He is in our lives. You are born with purpose and destiny, so *push* past the present and embrace your future. When we are in a state of perpetual disobedience, we will always miss the point. Never give God your leftovers; He has always given you His best! As we allow God's word to be the catalyst for our lives, He will alter our spirits and guide us to do better. And last, if we look at ourselves realistically through God's word, we will not only have a healthy relationships, but others will see His imprint on our lives too. Is all of this easy? No. Is it worth it? Yes, but remember it's a journey, not something that happens over night.

The Holy Spirit is the cleansing agent, and the Savior's blood is the spot remover. If you continually work out your salvation, you will remain in His will. Remaining in His will is always worth it. Be of good courage, take heart, and strive for excellence as you let God rub you the wrong way.

Printed in the United States
By Bookmasters